BIRMINGHAM

BACK TO THE
FIFTIES

Alton & Jo Douglas

Holiday crowds waiting for "The Cornishman", Snow Hill Station, 24th July 1954.

© 2003 Alton and Jo Douglas
ISBN 978 1 85858 234 4
Published by Brewin Books Ltd., Doric House, 56 Alcester Road, Studley, Warwickshire B80 7LG.
Printed by Warwick Printing Co. Ltd., Caswell Road, Leamington Spa CV31 1QD.
Layout by Alton and Jo Douglas
All Rights Reserved
3rd Impression March 2010

Hawthorn Road, Perry Barr, 5th May 1959.

Front Cover: The Bull Ring, April 1958.

C o n t e n t s

BREWIN BOOKS LTD

Doric House, 56 Alcester Road,
Studley, Warwickshire B80 7LG

Tel: 01527 854228 Fax: 01527 852746

Vat Registration No. 705 0077 73

Dear Nostalgic,

Why the fifties again? Well, just pause and take a look at the decade – the Festival of Britain, the King's departure, Everest, the Coronation – and that's only up to mid-1953! So many of us were teenagers then, and the publication of my autobiography, "The Original Alton Douglas", this year, has given a greater personal impetus to the project. Apart from the tasters mentioned, we've also included Villa winning the FA Cup, the news of the first ever satellite, acres of familiar scenes – need I go on? I won't spoil it because the whole purpose of our books is to lead you on a voyage of discovery – so, off you go – BACK TO THE FIFTIES.

Yours, in friendship,

Alton

American recording star, Al Martino, relaxes in the grounds of St Philip's Cathedral, 13th August 1956.

3

Icknield Street (with Camden Street on the right), Hockley, January 1950.

Buckingham Street, Hockley, 9th January 1950.

Stratford Road, with Weatheroak Road in sight, Sparkhill, March 1950.

The Lord Mayor, Ald. Hubert Humphreys and the Lady Mayoress, 1950.

5

The Boys' Brigade prepare to set out from St Cuthbert's Church, Cuthbert Road, Winson Green, c 1950.

Warwick Street, Highgate, 1950.

Ingestre Road/Stratford Road, Hall Green, 1950.

Adelaide Street, Highgate, 1950.

Great Charles Street/New Market Street, 1950.

BSA Tools Ltd. Cricket Club Dance, Market Hotel,
Station Street, 1950.

The Lord Mayor, Ald. A.P. Smith, meets members of the
Birmingham Consular Association, 20th June 1950.

The Rt. Hon. Anthony Eden takes the salute, as the British Legion march through Victoria Square, 2nd July 1950.

THE FOLLOWING BULLETIN WAS ISSUED FROM CLARENCE HOUSE THIS AFTERNOON: Her Royal Highness, the Princess Elizabeth, Duchess of Edinburgh, was safely delivered of a Princess at 11.50 a.m. to-day, at Clarence House. Her Royal Highness and her daughter are both doing well. Signed: William Gilliatt, John H. Peel, Vernon F. Hall and John Weir.

15/8/50

Mannequins for the night

At the Stirchley Pavilion on Tuesday, October 24th, four Tascos shop assistants acted as mannequins for the evening during the course of a showing of the Ivor Novello film *The Dancing Years*. The girls paraded in evening frocks taken from the mantles department stock. A packed house gave them a most enthusiastic reception.

Our picture shows the girls (Mrs. Betty Franklin, Miss Mollie Gibbs, Miss Jean Knight, and Mrs. Doreen Townsend) together with the Pavilion manager, Mr. Percy Freedman.

Hazelwell Lane, Stirchley, 1950.

B.S.A. **WINS**

SOLO
(W. NICHOLSON)

and

SIDECAR
(H. TOZER)

IN

British Experts Trial 1950

B.S.A. Cycles Ltd. Birmingham

Britain's Top Tunes

THIS list of the 20 best-selling songs for the week ended December 2 is supplied by the Popular Publishers' Committee of the Music Publishers' Association, Ltd.

1. RUDOLPH, THE RED-NOSED REINDEER (A) ...... Chappell
2. GOODNIGHT, IRENE (A).. Leeds
3. MONA LISA (A) .... New World
4. I TAUT I TAW A PUDDY TAT (A) .... Harms-Connelly
5. SAM'S SONG (A) ...... Sterling
6. HAVE I TOLD YOU LATELY THAT I LOVE YOU? (A) Leeds
7. BELOVED, BE FAITHFUL (A) .... Pickwick
8. AUTUMN LEAVES (F) .... Peter Maurice
9. SILVER DOLLAR (A) .... Merrin
10. CHRISTMAS IN KILLARNEY (A) .... Harms-Connelly
11. ASHES OF ROSES (A) .... Campbell Connelly
12. I ONLY SAW HIM ONCE (A) .... Unit
13. MY CHRISTMAS WISH (B) .... Michael Reine
14. ORANGE COLOURED SKY (A) .... Morris
15. IF I WERE A BLACKBIRD (B) .... Box and Cox
16. IF I LOVED YOU (A) Williamson
17. BEWITCHED (A) ...... Sterling
18. DADDY'S LITTLE GIRL (A) Yale
19. TZENA TZENA TZENA (A) Leeds
20. WE'LL KEEP A WELCOME (B) .... Edward Cox

A—American. B—British. F—French.

Jack Hayes, Marjorie Browne, Jack Stanford and Erica Yorke, at rehearsals for "Babes in the Wood" at the Theatre Royal, 18th December 1950. The poodle's name was Toffee!

Bullock Street/Proctor Street, Vauxhall, 1951.

Gooch Street, Highgate, 1951.

Birmingham Repertory Theatre, Station Street, 1951.
The current show was "Oliver Twist".

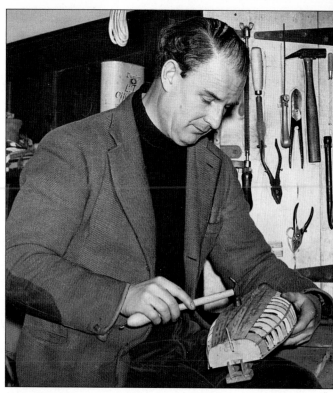

The Rt. Hon. Henry Usborne, MP for Yardley, tries his
hand at miniature boat-building, 18th February 1951.

The Steam Clock, Sherborne Street/Morville Street, Ladywood, 1951.

Dunlop Colts, winners of several trophies in the Works Soccer League, May 1951.

Lee Crescent, off Ryland Road, Edgbaston, 1951.

Spring Lane, Erdington, 1951.

FESTIVAL of BRITAIN IN BIRMINGHAM

PROGRAMME OF SHOWS AND EXHIBITIONS

APRIL

30—
May 11 **British Industries Fair** *Castle Bromwich*
Public Admission daily 2 p.m.—6 p.m. 2s. 6d.
Saturday May 5 — 9.30 a.m.—6 p.m. Reduced price 1s. 6d. for parties of 20 and over.

MAY

5 **Birmingham Horse Parade** *City Centre*
Parade through City Centre between 4 p.m. and 5 p.m.

7—26 Roy Fransen's **"Aqua Revue of 1951"**
(except Sunday) *Woodcock Street Baths*

8— **Exhibition of Water Colours, Drawings,**
June 2 **Pastels, Etchings etc.**
Royal Birmingham Society of Artists Gallery, New Street

8 & 9 **Festival of Movement and Dance** *Central Hall*

26 **Kings Norton and Northfield Horse Show**
Kings Norton, 10 a.m.

30— **Industrial Safety Exhibition** *Bingley Hall*
June 2

31 **Festival Demonstration** by the Women's League
of Health and Beauty *Central Hall, 7.30 p.m.*

JUNE

1 & 2 **Industrial Safety Exhibition** *Bingley Hall*

6 & 7 **Festival of Britain's Dances** presented by the
English Folk Dance & Song Society *Central Hall, 7 p.m.*

7, 8 **The Bingley Hall Festival Exhibition and**
& 9 **"Old Folks at Home Fair"** *Bingley Hall*
approx. 10 a.m.

9 **Veteran Car Rally** *Civic Centre*

9 **Physical Training Display** *Villa Park, 2.45 p.m.*
The display will be honoured by the presence of Her Royal
Highness The Princess Elizabeth.

9—16 **Festival of Britain Week** *Sheldon*

11—30 **Exhibition of Paintings** by Mrs. Fay Pomerance
Royal Birmingham Society of Artists Gallery, New Street

16 **Sea Cadet Corps Display** *Edgbaston Reservoir*

16 **Girl Guides Rally** *Highbury Park, 3 p.m.*

23 & **Festival of Cycling** *Dunlop Sports Grounds*
24

23 **Birmingham Settlement Festival Fete**
610 Kingstanding Road

24 **Bournville Jubilee Celebrations** *Bournville*
—30

JULY

During the month of July the Central Fire Station
will be open for inspection at 7 p.m. each Monday,
Tuesday, Thursday and Friday. Admission will
be by ticket only obtainable from the Central
Fire Station and from the Information Department,
Council House and 57 Corporation Street.

4, 11 **Demonstration by City Fire Service**
18 & 25 *Central Fire Station 3 p.m.*
Admission by ticket only obtainable from Central Fire Station
or Information Department, Council House and 57 Corporation
Street.

7 **Boy Scouts Rally** *Handsworth Park*

11— **Exhibition of English Tapestries**
Aug. 26 *Museum & Art Gallery*

11— **Festival of Britain Exhibition**
Aug. 11 *Royal Birmingham Society of Artists Gallery, New Street*

14 **Festival of Britain Harborne Horse Show**
Lightwoods Park 10.30 a.m.

14 **Kings Norton Carnival**
Cotteridge Park 2 p.m. — 10 p.m.

17, 18 **Physical Training Displays**
& 19 *Central Hall, 2.30 p.m. & 7 p.m.*

JULY 27 — AUGUST 18
EXHIBITION OF
RARE AND VALUABLE BOOKS
Central Library

The Exhibition will consist of about 250 of the
many treasures of the Birmingham Public Libraries

AUGUST

AUGUST 4 — 25
FESTIVAL OF BRITAIN
TRAVELLING EXHIBITION
Bingley Hall

Containing over 5,000 exhibits, this is the world's
largest transportable covered exhibition.

9 **Industrial Exhibition — "Birmingham, The**
onwards **Factory of Britain** *Newhall Street*

18 **Annual Rally of the Birmingham Street**
Savings Groups Committee *Highbury Park*

31 & **City of Birmingham Show**
Sept. 1 *Handsworth Park*
One of the most comprehensive shows in the country, comprising
Flower Show, Championship Dog Show, Horse Show, Honey
Show, Rabbit Show and Cage Bird Show. Variety entertainments
—Military Band Concerts, Firework Displays.

SEPTEMBER

1	City of Birmingham Show	Handsworth Park
5 6 & 7	Royal Air Forces Association Combined Services Tattoo	Alexander Sports Stadium, Perry Barr
26	Festival of Folk Dancing	Central Hall, 7 p.m.

The information contained in this leaflet was supplied by the organisers and no responsibility can be accepted for any alterations which may have been made since going to press.

Alan Brewin takes part in the Festival of Cycling, Dunlop Sports' Ground, 23rd June 1951. If the surname sounds familiar, Alan is our publisher!

One of the helicopters which operated a shuttle service between the short-lived base at Hay Mills and Elmdon Airport, Elmdon, June 1951.

15

St Vincent's Roman Catholic Church, Vauxhall Grove,
Vauxhall, c 1951.

Ashted Row, c 1951.

THE STATE OF THE PARTIES

	Gains	Losses	New House	Old House
CONSERVATIVES *(4 unopposed returns)*	23	1	319	298
LABOUR	2	22	293	314
LIBERAL	1	4	5	9
OTHERS	1	—	†3	4
			Total	625

†Others : 2 Irish Nationalists ; 1 Irish Labour.
There are still five results to come, including Barnsley, where polling day has been postponed to November 8

THE WAY VOTES WERE CAST

	Per Party 1951	1950	Per M.P. 1951 (approx.)	1950
CONSERVATIVE	13,665,595	12,501,983	42,800	41,800
LABOUR	13,877,922	13,295,736	47,400	42,300
LIBERAL	710,934	2,621,489	142,200	281,000
OTHERS	198,149	350,269	66,000	175,100

Electorate : 1951, 34,914,912 (82.7% voted).   Electorate : 1950, 34,269,764 (84% voted).

Daniell Memorial Hall, Hope Street, Highgate, December 1951.

The Congregational Chapel, Wheeler Street, Hockley, December 1951.

Barford Road Gardeners' Club Christmas Party, Rotton Park, 1951.

1952

Adelaide Street, Highgate, 1952.

Betty King and Elsie Newman (right) begin the day with a smile, 81 New Street, c 1952. The tobacconists was owned by
the St John family and was situated next to Dale, Forty and Co. Ltd.

The man of service

A BEREAVED nation mourns its King. There is sorrow in all our hearts. We loved him. And countless millions beyond the seas are sharers in our grief. His peoples and all who are linked with them in friendship.

The blow is heavier because we had hoped and believed that King George was on the way to recovery. The news shocked and stunned us. But to him the end came gently, peacefully. He passed away in his sleep. For him there was "no sadness of farewell"—only a deeper rest.

He died at Sandringham, the place that to him was home above all others. He had spent his last days amid scenes he had known since childhood, scenes filled with happy memories.

To the Royal Family we offer our deepest sympathy; especially to the Queen Mother for the loss of her dearly-beloved husband, to Queen Mary for the loss of a dearly-beloved son, and to the Queen and Princess Margaret for the loss of their dearly-beloved father.

It is more than a king we have lost. We have lost a man whose life was a proud record of devoted and unstinting service; who took the whole of his peoples into his care and who has died at a sadly early age because he would not spare himself in the task that came upon him.

Lambeth Road, Perry Barr, 25th March 1952.

Broad Street/King Alfred Place, 1952. Symphony Hall stands on this site now. At one time, the Prince of Wales Theatre formed the centrepiece (you can just see the remnants of its title).

Monument Grove, off Parker Street, Ladywood, 1952. Note the Anderson Shelter, still in use, as an allotment shed.

Five Ways, from the junction of Harborne Road/Calthorpe Road, 1st April 1952.

Cromwell Hall Anniversary Parade, Tudor Street, Winson Green, c 1952.

Golden Hillock Road, Small Heath, 28th April 1952.

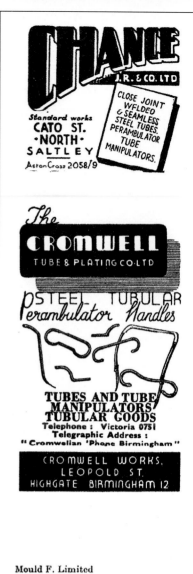

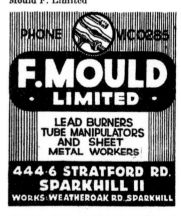

The Green/Pershore Road South/Wharf Road, Kings Norton, 27th May 1952.

Olton Boulevard East, Acocks Green, 16th June 1952.

The last tram leaves Selly Oak Depot with the Lord Mayor, Ald. W.T. Bowen, at the controls, 5th July 1952.

The last tram along the Pershore Road route, 5th July 1952.

Birmingham Diocesan
Church of England Temperance Society.

CERTIFICATE OF MERIT

awarded to

Joyce Lockwood

Primary   Division Dudley Road   School

Subject : *"The Four Cardinal Virtues."*

SECOND CLASS   JULY. 1952

Prevention
is Better
than Cure

A. Beaumont,   Chairman

Alfred Phillips,   Secretary

"Add to your Faith, Virtue ; and to Virtue, Knowledge ; and to Knowledge, Temperance."

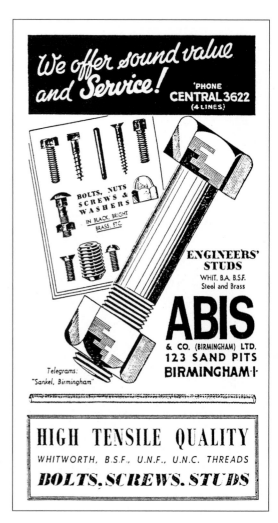

The Onion Fair, Serpentine Ground, Aston, 1952.

Frances Watson sets out her stall at the Onion Fair, 27th September 1952.

Her Majesty, The Queen, opens Birmingham's Water Department's Clarewen Dam, 23rd October 1952.

Looking towards Saltley from Cato Street, 12th December 1952.

The front cloth for the Alexandra Theatre's production of "Dick Whittington", December 1952.
Painted by Rex Spencer, this was always a favourite of Derek Salberg's.

Jean Inglis, who played the title
role of Dick Whittington.

Ida Shepley as the
Queen of Cantata.

Aston Brook Street, 13th January 1953.

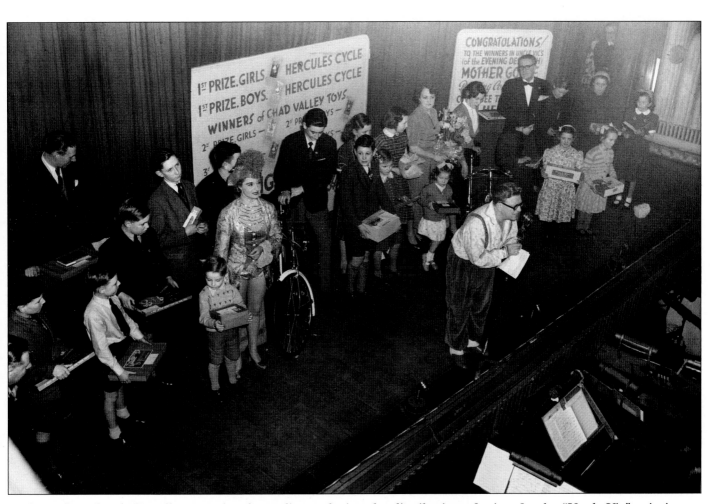

Comedian, Sandy Powell, entertains the audience during the distribution of prizes for the "Uncle Vic" painting competition, Aston Hippodrome, 20th January 1953.

Jerrys Lane, Erdington, 1953.

Sweet rationing finally comes to an end, 4th February 1953. It had actually ended in 1949 but the enormous demand meant that it had to be re-introduced for a further four years.

Taking up the tram lines, Birchfield Road, Perry Barr, 4th March 1953.

Gravelly Lane, with Station Road on the left, Erdington, 28th May 1953.

Wallace Lawler, the Liberal candidate for Dudley, responds to hecklers, in a car park by the Bull Ring, 22nd March 1953. In time he became the MP for Ladywood.

HILLARY DOES IT

*G*LORIOUS *Coronation Day news! Everest—Everest the unconquerable — has been conquered. And conquered by men of British blood and breed.*

The news came late last night that Edmund Hillary and the Sherpa guide, Tensing, of Colonel Hunt's expedition had climbed to the summit of Earth's highest peak, 29,002 feet high.

Queen Elizabeth the Second, resting on the eve of her crowning, was immediately told that this brightest jewel of courage and endurance had been added to the Crown of British endeavour. It is understood that a message of royal congratulation was sent to the climbers.

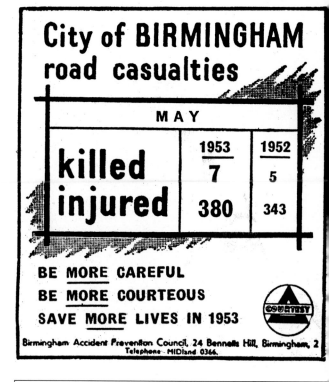

Albert Road, Stechford, May 1953.

THE
ORDER OF DIVINE SERVICE
FOR
TRINITY ·SUNDAY 31 MAY 1953
BEING THE SUNDAY PRECEDING
HER MAJESTY'S
CORONATION
RECOMMENDED FOR USE IN ALL
CHURCHES OF THE
CHURCH OF ENGLAND

ISSUED BY COMMAND OF THE QUEEN

Kitchener Road, Selly Park, June 1953.

Coronation decorations, Victoria Square, June 1953.

CITY OF BIRMINGHAM

CORONATION

OF

HER MAJESTY QUEEN ELIZABETH II

2ND JUNE 1953

*PROGRAMME OF
CELEBRATIONS*

PRODUCED AND PUBLISHED FOR THE
CORONATION CELEBRATIONS COMMITTEE BY THE
CITY OF BIRMINGHAM INFORMATION DEPARTMENT

PRICE - SIXPENCE

WHIT-MONDAY, 25th MAY

2.30 p.m.	"The Birmingham Mail" Coronation Air Display	ELMDON AIRPORT *for details see p. 7*

SUNDAY, 31st MAY

11 a.m.	Civic Coronation Service	THE CATHEDRAL *for details see p.4*
7.30 p.m.	Orchestral Concert: City of Birmingham Symphony Orchestra *Solo Violin:* YEHUDI MENUHIN	TOWN HALL *for details see p.8*

MONDAY, 1st JUNE

1.15 p.m.	Organ Recital by Dr. Harold Darke	TOWN HALL *for details see p.9*
5.15 p.m.	Open Air Religious Service	VICTORIA SQUARE *for details see p.4*
7 p.m.	Concert by B.B.C. Midland Light Orchestra	TOWN HALL *for details see p.9*

TUESDAY, 2nd JUNE   CORONATION DAY

10 a.m. onwards	Rediffusion of B.B.C. Television programme (Organised by Birmingham Post and Mail Ltd.)	TOWN HALL AND MIDLAND INSTITUTE
10.26 a.m.	Royal Salute will be fired	CANNON HILL PARK *for details see p. 14*
Afternoon & Evening	Children's Entertainments in various Parks and Recreation Grounds	*for details see p.18-19*
Afternoon	Band Concerts, Concert Parties, etc. in various parks	*for details see p.15-17*
Evening	Band Concerts, Concert Parties and Firework displays in various parks	*for details see p.15-19 and 29*

WEDNESDAY, 3rd JUNE

1.15 p.m.	Organ Recital by the City Organist, Dr. G. Thalben-Ball	TOWN HALL *for details see p.10*
7.30 p.m.	Choral and Orchestral Concert by the Birmingham Choral Union with the City of Birmingham Symphony Orchestra. *Solo Pianoforte:* Phyllis Sellick	TOWN HALL *for details see p.10*

THURSDAY, 4th JUNE

1.10 p.m.	Recital of Chamber Music by the Element String Quartet	ART GALLERY
7 p.m.	Children's Concert: The Birmingham Children's Choir with a section of the City of Birmingham Symphony Orchestra	TOWN HALL *for details see p.10*
7.30 p.m.	Recital of Music by the Birmingham Bach Society Choir and Orchestra	THE CATHEDRAL *for details see p.11*

FRIDAY, 5th JUNE

1.10 p.m.	Recital of Chamber Music	ART GALLERY *for details see p.11*
8 p.m.— midnight	Old Time Dance with Leonard Hayes and his Orchestra	TOWN HALL *for details see p.13*

SATURDAY, 6th JUNE

2 p.m.	Warwickshire County A.A.A. Track and Field Events Championships	PERRY BARR *for details see p.7*
2.45 p.m.	Ceremonial Parade and March Past	CITY CENTRE *for details see p.20-23*
7.30 p.m.	Popular Concert by the City of Birmingham Symphony Orchestra	TOWN HALL *for details see p.11*
7.30 p.m.	Tollefson, the Accordion virtuoso and the George Clay Accordion Band	ASTON PARK *for details see p.15*
7.30 p.m.	Ted Heath and His Music	CANNON HILL PARK *for details see p.15*
7.30 p.m.	Jack Parnell and his Music Makers	HANDSWORTH PARK *for details see p.16*
7.30 p.m.	The National Band of New Zealand	LIGHTWOODS PARK *for details see p.16*
7.30 p.m.	Band of H.M. Coldstream Guards	SMALL HEATH PARK *for details see p.17*
7.30 p.m.	The Royal Artillery Mounted Band and the Leicester Girls Choir	WARD END PARK *for details see p.17*
10.0 p.m.	Firework Displays in Aston Park, Cannon Hill Park, Handsworth Park, Lightwoods Park, Small Heath Park and Ward End Park The firework displays will be preceded by Community Singing	

SUNDAY, 7th JUNE

7.30 p.m.	Choral and Orchestral Concert by the City of Birmingham Choir with the City of Birmingham Symphony Orchestra	TOWN HALL *for details see p. 12*

MONDAY, 8th JUNE

12.30 p.m.	Open Air Concert by the National Band of New Zealand	CIVIC CENTRE
7.30 p.m.	Concert by the National Band of New Zealand	TOWN HALL

TUESDAY, 9th JUNE

7.30 p.m.	Popular Concert by the Birmingham Philharmonic Orchestra	TOWN HALL *for details see p.12*

THURSDAY, 11th JUNE

7.30 p.m.	Organ Recital by the City Organist, Dr. G. Thalben-Ball	TOWN HALL *for details see p.13*

FRIDAY, 12th JUNE

7.30 p.m.	The Humphrey Lyttelton Jazz Show	TOWN HALL

SATURDAY, 13th JUNE

8 p.m.— 11.30 p.m.	Coronation Barn Dance	TOWN HALL *for details see p.13*

CORONATION AIR DISPLAY

Birmingham's Coronation Air Display, sponsored by "The Birmingham Mail" in conjunction with the Midland Aero Club Ltd., will be held at Elmdon Airport on Whit. Monday, May 25, commencing at 2.30 p.m. The programme of spectacular flying events and ground exhibition includes a fly past of high speed aircraft in service with the Royal Air Force.

Admission: *Public enclosure* **1s.** *Special enclosure* **5s. extra.** Refreshments and ample car parking facilities.

WARWICKSHIRE COUNTY AMATEUR ATHLETIC ASSOCIATION

TRACK AND FIELD EVENTS CHAMPIONSHIPS, Alexander Sports Ground, Perry Barr, June 6 at 2 p.m. The City of Birmingham Coronation Celebrations Committee have presented a trophy for annual competition in the One Mile Flat Race.

THE eyes through which 125 million television viewers in Europe and America will see the bulk of the Abbey ceremony today belong to Dennis Montague, 35 - year - old senior cameraman of the B.B.C.'s mobile TV unit based on Birmingham.

THE EYES closed early last night, and opened at 4 a.m. today to face their sternest test in seven years of looking at life and events through the view-finder of a camera for the ever-growing army of viewers.

Out on loan

THE EYES were lucky to be chosen for the job. It was a combination of circumstances. "Monty" Montague happened to work one of the newest cameras in B.B.C. service; he happened to combine experience with a height of 5ft. 7in., and it was necessary not to have a tall man hunched into the low camera cubicle high up there above the Coronation Theatre.

Members of Kings Norton Youth Fellowship, prior to demonstration of Scottish dancing, Coronation garden party, Kings Norton Vicarage.

THE VOICE OF BRITAIN RANG OUT ONCE MORE PROUDLY THROUGH THE WORLD, RAISED IN TRIUMPHANT SONG, AS QUEEN ELIZABETH WAS CROWNED IN WESTMINSTER ABBEY YESTERDAY.

And a new sun shone in this reawakened land—the burning radiance of fifty million faces—shaming the sun which, after briefly gracing the Abbey, was now hiding.

Never in all its history has London seen such a sight. The greatest city in the world was crowned with gold and paved with happy faces.

3/6/63

LONG MAY SHE REIGN

IN the stark simplicities of life and death, monarchs are like other mortals. But in one thing they are unique. At their crowning and sacring they become beings set apart. Only they can be central figures in the mystery of Coronation.

Those who have been thus elected and anointed are few indeed among the multitudes of the human race. Of these few only one today is the subject of a rite which goes back to the misty past and has preserved inviolate its immemorial forms and customs.

That one is our sovereign lady QUEEN ELIZABETH II. Today she will become the 39th monarch to be crowned in the Abbey church which, in its original shape, was consecrated 888 years ago.

2/6/53

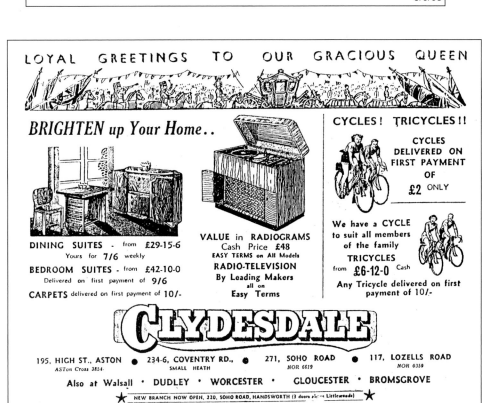

Bishop Street, Highgate, 1953.

Tory MP, Edith Pitt, is chaired by her supporters, after winning the Edgbaston seat, 3rd July 1953.

Windsor Arcade, 1st August 1953.

T/S Vernon's Sea Cadets, Edgbaston Reservoir, 1953. They had just won the Efficiency Pendant for the fifth successive year.

Max Wall, appearing in "Cap and Belles", Hippodrome, 14th September 1953.

Mr. P. Goode demonstrates the new Crescent Theatre lighting board, Cambridge Street, 26th September 1953.

The Rt. Hon. Cecil Poole, MP for Perry Barr, 1953.

Kings Norton Station, 26th September 1953.

Stan Laurel and Oliver Hardy, on stage at the
Hippodrome, 30th November 1953.

Norman Evans, playing Dame, tries to tempt Betty
Jumel, Theatre Royal, Christmas 1953.

1954

Marsh Lane/Slade Road, Erdington, 15th January 1954.

High Street, with the News Theatre on the left, 24th February 1954.

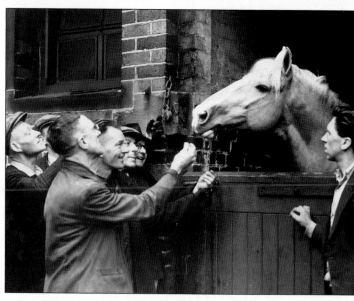

– but Trigger prefers to meet his fans from the comfort of his stable in Holliday Street.

Western star, Roy Rogers, takes his horse up to check the bedrooms at the Queen's Hotel, 1st March 1954.

Richard and Barbara Lyon, Bebe Daniels and Ben Lyon, stars of the radio and stage show, "Life With The Lyons", Grand Hotel, 1st March 1954.

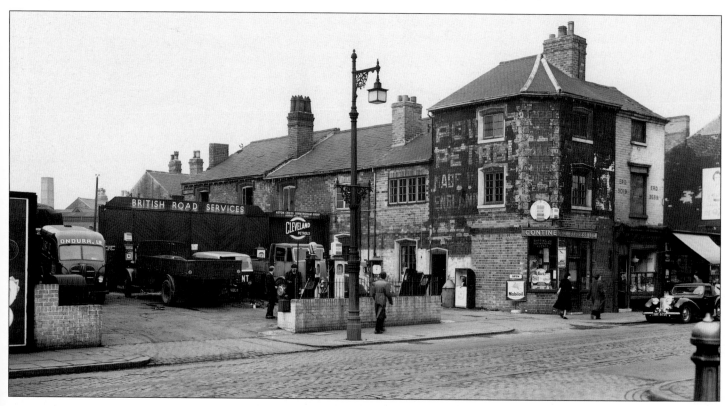

Lichfield Road, Aston, 3rd March 1954.

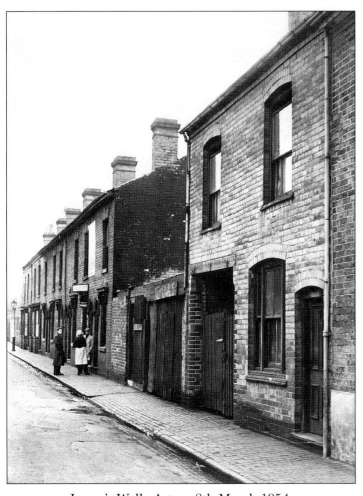

Lover's Walk, Aston, 8th March 1954.

"Little Lambs Eat Ivy", Kings Norton Youth Fellowship,
Saracen's Head, The Green, 20th May 1954.

Paradise Street/Suffolk Street, 1954.

Gravelly Hill North, Erdington, 21st May 1954.

Great Charles Street, 1954.

College Road, Kingstanding, 14th June 1954.

BIRMINGHAM AND MIDLAND INSTITUTE
1954
CENTENARY YEAR

On the Centenary of the Institute's Act of Incorporation the Council invites

Miss J.M. Lockwood

to a Service of Thanksgiving and Rededication at Birmingham Cathedral by kind permission of the Provost on Saturday, 3rd July, 1954, at 10 a.m. when the preacher will be the Lord Bishop of Birmingham

R.S.V.P. ON CARD ENCLOSED

Kingsbury Road, Erdington, 1954.

Raddlebarn Road,
Bournville, 1954.

Steelhouse Lane, with Newton Street on the left, 25th August 1954.

Weaman Street/Steelhouse Lane, 1954.

45

Central Fire Station, c 1953.

Sir Edward Boyle, Parliamentary Secretary, Ministry of
Supply and Conservative MP for Handsworth (left) visits
the BSA, Kings Heath, 14th September 1954.

Ruby Murray.

Alma Cogan.

Just two of the singers who appeared at the Hippodrome in 1954.

Holly Lane, Erdington, 11th October 1954.

Soho Hill, Handsworth, 18th October 1954.

Part of the Sea Cadets' Parade, St Philip's,
25th October 1954.

Temple Row, with Cherry Street on the extreme left, 1954.

Lichfield Road, with Bourne Road, left of centre, Aston, 3rd November 1954.

Rawlins Street, Ladywood, 1954.

"Quiet Weekend", St Nicolas Amateur Dramatic Society, Saracen's Head, Kings Norton, 21st November 1954.

Bull Street, 9th December 1954.

Great Western Arcade, 23rd December 1954.

The Rt. Hon. Julius Silverman, Labour
MP for Erdington, 1955.

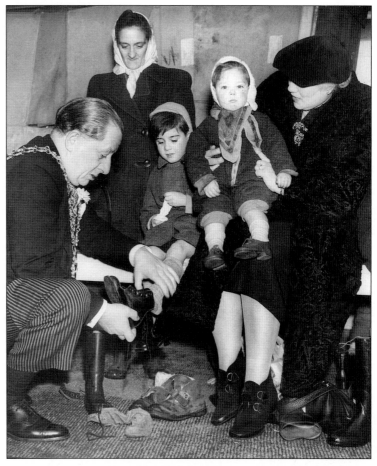

The annual distribution of boots and shoes to needy
children, on behalf of the Birmingham Mail Christmas Tree
Fund, is made by the Lord Mayor, Ald. J.R. Balmer,
14th January 1955.

W. Canning and Co. Ltd., (makers of electro-platers' and polishers' plant and material),
Great Hampton Street, Hockley, 1955.

Fazeley Street, 1955.

Upper Dean Street/Gloucester Street, 8th February 1955.

Hurst Street, with Thorp Street on the right, 22nd February 1955.

Temple Row, 3rd March 1955.

Bull Street, 3rd March 1955.

The fire brigade tackle the blaze at the Halford Cycle Co. Ltd.,
Lancaster Street/Corporation Street, 12th March 1955.

Staff from Birmingham Museum and Art Gallery struggle with Henry Moore's statue
"The Warrior", 17th March 1955.

Nechells Place, 1955.

Bristol Road South, with the Black Horse pub on the left, Northfield, 27th April 1955.

Six Ways, Erdington, with Gravelly Hill North on the right of our picture, 25th May 1955.

Orphanage Road, Erdington, 1955.

Longmore Road, Balsall Heath, 28th June 1955.

56

Ryland Street, Edgbaston, 27th July 1955.

C&A, Corporation Street, 27th August 1955. Beatties is now on this site.

The Birmingham Hospital Saturday Fund.

KEWSTOKE
CONVALESCENT HOME FOR WOMEN,
SAND BAY, WESTON-SUPER-MARE.

OFFICES : 8-9, LUDGATE HILL, BIRMINGHAM, 3.
Telephone: CENtral 3275.

Owing to restricted accommodation at these offices when patients are travelling, it is requested that at time of departure you shall not be accompanied by more than one person.

26 AUG 1955

Dear Madam,

Arrangements have been made for your admission to the Kewstoke Convalescent Home on Monday next and a motor coach will leave the offices of the Fund at **2-0 p.m.** prompt.

Please be at 8-9, Ludgate Hill, at **1-30 p.m.** to obtain admission card and pay the required return fare of **£1.**

If you should be unable to go, please advise me by telephone, if possible, or by return of post, otherwise you will forfeit your right to go to the Home.

Yours truly,
THE SECRETARY.

In case of further reference please quote

No. 104

Hob Moor Road, Small Heath, 21st November 1955.

PRINCESS MARGARET ISSUED THE FOLLOWING PERSONAL MESSAGE FROM HER HOME, CLARENCE HOUSE, LAST NIGHT :

I would like it to be known that I have decided not to marry Group-Captain Peter Townsend.

I have been aware that, subject to my renouncing my rights of succession, it might have been possible for me to contract a civil marriage.

But, mindful of the Church's teaching that Christian marriage is indissoluble, and conscious of my duty to the Commonwealth, I have resolved to put these considerations before any others.

I have reached this decision entirely alone, and in doing so I have been strengthened by the unfailing support and devotion of Group-Captain Townsend.

I am deeply grateful for the concern of all those who have constantly prayed for my happiness.

The message was dated Monday, Oct. 31 and was signed "Margaret."

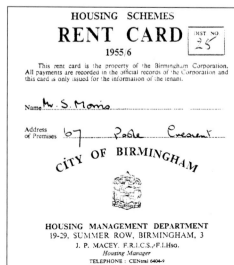

Berkeley Street, with Holliday Street in sight, 28th December 1955.

Thorp Street/Horse Fair, December 1955.

1956

Elkington Street School Infants, with Mrs. Cope, Aston, 1956.

Elkington Street School Juniors, with Mrs. Cropper, Aston, 1956.

The first short wave wireless call to the city's new radio taxi service is made by the Lord Mayor, Ald. A.L. Gibson, 1st February 1956.

Preparing for the launch of ITV transmissions, Alpha Studios, Aston, 17th February 1956.

Country and Western singer, Slim Whitman, pays a visit to Queen Elizabeth Hospital to record a programme for hospital patients, 19th March 1956. He was appearing at the Hippodrome for the week.

Station Road, Erdington, March 1956.

Grange Road/Alcester Road South, Kings Heath, 1956.

Jerry Desmonde (centre) hosting the Midland ITV quiz show, "Hit the Limit", discusses the script with producer Reg Watson and programme assistant Pauline Tyler, 27th March 1956. The show was coming from Bingley Hall.

Coventry Road, at the point where it joins Green Lane on our immediate right, Small Heath, 1956.

Bull Street, March 1956.

ADELPHI, Hay Mills (A.B.C.). "Trial" (A), "Johnny You're Wanted" (A). Sunday: "California Conquest" (U).

ALBION, New Inns, H'worth. "The Last Frontier" (A). "Gamma People" (A). Sun.: "8 Iron Men" (A).

ALHAMBRA, Moseley Road (ABC).—"Trial" (A), "Johnny You're Wanted" (A). Sun.: "The Brigand" (U).

APOLLO, Tyburn Rd. ERD. 0834. "The Purple Mask" (U), "One Good Turn" (U). L.P. 7. S.: 'Fort Algiers' U.

ATLAS, Stechford. STE. 2206. "Blue & the Gold" (U), "African Fury" (U). "Adventures of Buccaneers" (U).

BEACON, Gt. Barr.—C/S. "Adventures of Quentin Durward" U. "Double Cross" U. S.: "High Venture" A.

BEAUFORT. — C/S. "The Lieutenant Wore Skirts" (U), "Las Vegas Shakedown" A. S.: "Boots Malone" U

BIRCHFIELD. Cont. 2.0.— "Private's Progress" (U), "Fangs of the Wild" U. S.: "California Conquest" U

CAPITOL—Fess Parker, "Davy Crockett" (U), "Tons of Trouble" (U). Sun.: "Great Flamarion" (U).

CARLTON. Sou. 0861.—Dirk Bogarde, "Simba" (A), "Destry" (A). Sun.: "Murder Without Crime" (A).

CASTLE. CAS. 2425.—"To Hell & Back" (A), "Square Jungle" (A). Sun.: "Mask of the Avenger" (U).

CLIFTON, Gt. Barr.—Tech. "Davy Crockett" (U), "Tons of Trouble" (U) S.: "It's a Grand Life" (U).

CORONET.—"Man With the Golden Arm" (x), Supp. adults only. Sun.: "Thief of Damascus" (U).

CROWN, Ladywood (A.B.C.).— Fess Parker, B. Ebson, "Davy Crockett" (U), Tech. "Tons of Trouble" (U).

DANILO, Quinton. WOO. 2562. "Virgin Queen" (U), "Little Red Monkey" (A). S. "Female on the Beach" (A).

EDGBASTON, Monument Rd. (ABCA).—"Adventures of Quentin Durward" U, Sup U. S.: "Plunder of the Sun" U

ELITE, H'worth.—"The Glen Miller Story" (U), "The Blue Lamp" (A); Sun.: "Curtain Up" (U)

EMPIRE. SME. 0757.—Tech. Doris Day, "CALAMITY JANE" U; Jane Wyman, "Private Detective" (A)

EMPRESS, Sutton (A.B.C.).— "DAVY CROCKETT" (U), "Tons of Trouble" (U); S.: "Secret Interlude" (A)

ERA, Bordesley Grn. VIC. 0543. Martin & Lewis, "Artists and Models" U, Full Supp. S.: 'Bonadventure' A.

ESSOLDO, Longbridge—"John and Julie" U, "Under the Caribbean" (U). Sun.: "Once a Thief" (A).

GAIETY, Coleshill St. (ABC). Fess Parker, "DAVY CROCKETT" (U), Tech.: "Tons of Trouble" (U)

GAUMONT. SME. 0950.— "Davy Crockett" (U); "Tons of Trouble" (U); Sun.: "Who Done It?" (U)

GRAND, Alum Rock.—William Holden, "Union Station" (A), "Dust & Gold" (U). S.: "Thief of Damascus" (U).

GRANGE.—T. Ewell, "The Lieutenant Wore Skirts" (U) "Rocket Man" (U) S.: "Prince of Pirates" (U).

GROVE, Dudley Road.—"Man with the Golden Arm" (x) Supp. (U). Adults only. S.: "Capt. Blood Fugitive" (U).

IMPERIAL, Moseley Rd. (ABC). Fess Parker, 'Davy Crockett' U, 'Tons of Trouble' U. Sun.: "Montana Belle" U.

KING'S NORTON. KIN. 1079. 'Davy Crockett' (U) 'Tons of Trouble' (U) LP. 7.15. S.: "High Venture" (a).

KINGSTON. — Fess Parker, "Davy Crockett" (U) Sun.: "All Ashore" (a) Tech

KINGSWAY. HIG. 1352.— 'Davy Crockett' (U) 'Tons of Trouble' (U) LP. 7.18. Sun.: "7 Cities of Gold" (U)

LUXOR.—Jane Wyman, "All That Heaven Allows" (U), "Hornets Nest" (U) Sun.: "The Big Cat" (U).

LYRIC, Parade. — "Jumping for Joy" (U); "Kettles in the Ozarks" (U). Sun: "Anne of the Indies" (U)

MAJESTIC, Bearwood.—"The Tender Trap" (U). "Las Vegas Shakedown" (A). Sun.: "After Midnight" (A)

MAYFAIR, Perry Common.— "The Colditz Story" (U); "Room In the House" (U). S.: "The Milkman" (A)

MAYPOLE. MAY. 2051. Fri. 5.30 —"Man with the Golden Arm" (x); Adults only. S.: "Dangerous Crossing" (A)

MOSELEY P.H—A Ray, "The Gentle Sergeant" (U); "Dangerous Cargo" (U). S.: "Perilous Journey" (A).

NEWTOWN PALACE.—"Joe Macbeth" (A); "Duel on the Mississippi" (U). S.: "Remember That Face" (U).

NORTHFIELD. PRI. 1463.— Glenn Ford, "Trial" (A); "Little Red Monkey" A. S.: "Ghost of St Michael's" U

OAK, Selly Oak (A.B.C.). "Man With the Golden Arm" (X). "Woman They Almost Lynched" (U).

ODEON, Blackheath. — C/S. Tech. J. Ferrer, 'Cockleshell Heroes' (U). "The Crooked Web" (U). L.P. 7.15.

ODEON, Kingstanding. SUT. 2551—'Picnic' (a) 'The Nebraskan' (a) LP. /. S.: 'Up Front' (U) Supp. (a).

ODEON, Perry Barr. Cont. 2.5 "Man With the Golden Arm" (x) Supp (U). Adults only. S.: "Up Front" (A)

ODEON, Shirley. Cont. 1.50— "Man With the Golden Arm" (x) Supp (U). Adults only. S.: "Secret Four" (U)

ODEON, Sutton Cont. 2.0.— "Man With the Golden Arm" (x) Supp (U). Adults only. S.: "Backlash" (U)

ODEON, Warley. Cont. 2.0.— "Man With the Golden Arm" (x) Supp U. Adults only. S.: 'Laughter in Paradise' U

OLTON—Fess Parker, "Davy Crockett" (U); "Tons of Trouble" (U); Sunday: "Dark Page" (A)

ORIENT, Aston (A.B.C.).— "Adventures of Quentin Durward" U. "Double Cross" U; S: "Above & Beyond" A

PALACE, Erdington (A.B.C.).— "Man With the Golden Arm" (X); Supp., adults only. S. "Crippl eCreek" (U).

PALLADIUM, Hockley (ABC). "Man With the Golden Arm" (X); None Under 16; S. "Behave Yourself" A

PAVILION, Stirchley (A.B.C.). "Adventures of Quentin Durward" U, Col.; S. "Everything I Have is Yours" U

PAVILION, Wylde Grn. (ABC) "Adventures of Quentin Durward" U; "Double Cross" U; S. 'Golden Earrings' A

PICCADILLY, Sparkbk. (ABC) "Man With the Golden Arm" (X); Full Suppt., adults only; S. "Iron Man" U

PICTURE House, Aston Cross (ABC). 'Storm Over the Nile' U; 'Mysterious Bullet' U; S. Texas Carnival U

PICTURE House, Erd. (ABC). 'Wizard o, Oz" (U), "The Glass Slipper" (U) Sun.: "Flame of Araby" (U).

PICTURE House, Harborne.— "Davy Crockett" (U) "Tons of Trouble" (U). L.P. 7. S.: "Corvette 225" (U).

PLAZA, Stockland Grn. Cont. 2. "Lost" (a) "Star in the Dust" (U) LP. 7.15. S.: "Great Missouri Raid" (a)

PRINCES, SME. 0221.—"Man With the Golden Arm" (x) Supp. A Adults only. S.: "El Paso" (U)

REGAL, Handsworth (A.B.C.). 'Adventures of Quentin Durward' (U) 'Doublecross' (U). S.: "Tangier" (U)

RIALTO, Hall Grn. SPR. 1270. "Davy Crockett" (U) "Tons of Trouble" (U) S.: "The Last Outpost" (U) Supp. A

RITZ, Bordesley Grn. (A.B.C.) "Seminole Uprising" (U), "Not So Dusty" (U) S.: "The Big Trees" (a).

ROBIN Hood, Hall Grn. (ABC) 'The Left Hand of God' (a) 'Pick Up on South Street' (a) S.: 'Worms Eye View' (U)

ROCK, Alum Rock.—"Man with the Golden Arm" (x) "Night Visitor" (a) Adults only S.: "Iron Man" (a)

ROOKERY, H'worth. NOR. 0691 "To Catch a Thief" (A); "3-Cornered Fate" A, LP 7.10. S.: "The Card" U

ROYALTY, Harborne (ABC) 'Demetrius & Gladiators' A; 'Pick-up on South Street' A; S. 'Winchester 73' U

RUBERY. RUBERY 193.—Jack Hawkins, 'Malta Story' U; "Tumble Weed" U. LP 7.25; S. "Flying Missile" U

SAVOY, King's Norton.—C/S. Tech. 'The Last Frontier' A; 'Gamma People' A; Sun. 'Laughter in Paradise' U

SHELDON. — Sheree North, "Lieutenant Wore Skirts" (U). C/S; "Fixed Bayonets" (A); Sun. "Outcast" U

SOLIHULL, SOL. 0398—Janette Scott, "Now & Forever" (U), Tech.; "Bread, Love & Jealousy" (A)

SPRINGFIELD, Stratford Rd. "YANKEE PASHA" (U); "Cimarron Kid" (U); S. "The Saint's Return" (U)

TIVOLI—Walt Disney's "Davy Crockett" (U) Tech.; "Tons of Money" (U). Sun.: "Angel Face" (A).

TUDOR, King's Heath (ABC). Geo. Montgomery, "SEMINOLE UPRISING" (U), Tech., "Not So Dusty" U

TYSELEY.—"The Sea Chase" (U), "Cattle Town" (U). S.: "Marching Along" (U).

VICTORIA. EAS. 0479.—C/S. Tech., "Valley of Fury" (U); "Forbidden" (A). S. "The Hasty Heart" (U)

VILLA CROSS. NOR. 0607.— "Davy Crockett" (U); "Tons of Trouble" (U) S.: "Toughest Man in Arizona" (U)

WALDORF. Sparkbrook.— 'Magnificent Obsession' (U); "A & C. Meet the Mummy" U. S. 'Viva Zapata' (A)

WARWICK. ACO. 0766.— "Now & Forever" (U); "Love, Bread & Jealousy" (A). Sun. "Red River" U

WEOLEY CASTLE—Norman Wisdom, "Man of the Moment" (U); "One Way Out" (U). L.P. 7.35.

WINSON GREEN, Car Park. "Storm Over the Nile" (U); "Life at Stake" (A). Sun.: "After Midnight" (A).

Film star, Fess Parker, in his guise as Davy Crockett, visits the Evening Despatch, 17th April 1956.

The Rt. Hon. Percy Shurmer, Labour MP for Sparkbrook, signs autographs for the pupils of Formans Road Secondary Modern School. House of Commons, 2nd May 1956.

The Three Magpies Bowling team, from Shirley Road, Hall Green, on a day trip to Blackpool, c 1956.

Edward Road, Balsall Heath, 1956.

Cromwell Hall Sunday School outing to The Lickeys, 1956.

Singing star, Yana, with her poodle "Toulouse Lautrec",
ITV canteen, Aston, 21st June 1956.

Bristol Road South, Northfield, 1956.

THE REFUSAL OF PRESIDENT NASSER TO NEGOTIATE ON THE BASIS SUGGESTED BY THE 18 NATIONS AT THE SUEZ CONFERENCE CREATED A VERY GRAVE SITUATION.

This was stated in an official communique from No. 10 Downing-street to-day after the meeting between the British and French leaders.

Four people took part in the talks to-day, which lasted three hours 20 minutes.

They were Sir Anthony Eden, Mr. Selwyn Lloyd, M. Mollet, the French Prime Minister, and M. Pineau, the French Foreign Minister.

11.9.56

Birmingham Co-operative Society Ltd., workshops, Ashted Row, Nechells Green, 28th August 1956.

Church Lane/Witton Lane, 1956.

More work goes on at the Big Top area, High Street/Bull Ring, 1956.

Turpin meets Italian

Randolph Turpin (Leamington), the British light - heavyweight champion, will have his next contest at the Sportsdrome, Birmingham, on Monday, October 28, when he meets Sergio Burchi, 25-year-old Italian light-heavyweight, who has won 17 of his 22 fights since he started professional boxing in 1954.

Golden Hillock Road, Small Heath, 1956.

Rudolph Schwarz with the City of Birmingham Orchestra, Town Hall, 1956.

BSA Tools Dept., Sales Office party, c 1956.

The sound of recorders accompanies the carol singing at St. Philip's,
14th December 1956.

The Lord Mayor, Ald. E.W. Apps, goes under "London Bridge" at the Council House Children's Christmas Party, 14th January 1957.

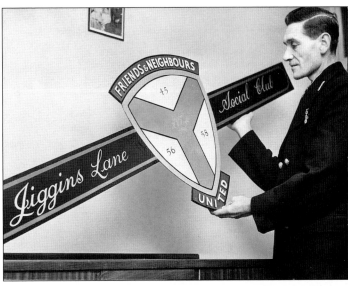

Mr. H.W. Knight holds up the crest of the Jiggins Lane Social Club, prior to their first social function at Harborne, 29th January 1957. The Bartley Green club was formed by residents in the new six-storey blocks of flats and Mr. Knight was the curator.

Dale End, January 1957.

Green Lane/Fourth Avenue, Small Heath, 15th February 1957.

H. A. BROOKS | **SCRAP MERCHANT** | Buyer of IRON, STEEL and NON-FERROUS METALS

DOROTHY ROAD, off WHARF ROAD, TYSELEY, BIRMINGHAM 11
Telephone: ACO. 3591

Park Road, Handsworth, 1957.

Holloway Head/Speaking Stile Walk, Edgbaston,
20th February 1957.

Singer and bandleader, Ray Ellington, appears at the Lord
Mayor's "Bob a Nob" jazz concert, Town Hall,
23rd February 1957.

F.A. CUP SEMI-FINALS 1957·ASTON VILLA - BIRMINGHAM CITY - WEST BROMWICH ALBION

Back row: R. Graham, (Albion trainer), J. Sanders, D. Pace, J. Dugdale, W. Moore (Villa trainer), P. Saward, G. Merrick, R. Shaw (Birmingham City coach).
Second row: F. Griffin, D. Howe, W. Myerscough, J. Sewell, T. Birch, P. McParland, K. O. Roberts, B. Orritt, J. Newman, G. Clarke (Albion assistant trainer).
Third row: A. Turner (Birmingham City manager), J. Kennedy, L. Millard, J. Dudley, P. Aldis, S. Lynn, N. Sims, G. Astall, J. Watts, P. Murphy, V. Buckingham (Albion team manager). *Fourth row:* E. Houghton (Villa manager), R. Horobin, M. Setters, R. Allen, W. Baxter, S. Crowther, L. Smith, N. Kinsey, T. Smith, K. Green.
Front row: R. Robson, B. Whitehouse, D. Kevan, R. Barlow, J. Dixon, R. Warhurst, E. Brown, J. Hall, A. Govan.

Alvechurch Road, West Heath, 1957.

Kettlehouse Road, Kingstanding, 1957.

Johnny Dixon collects the FA Cup from Her Majesty, The Queen, after Aston Villa had beaten Manchester United 2–1, Villa Park, 4th May 1957.

Warwick Road, Acocks Green, 1957.

Singer Frankie Vaughan, signs happily away for the fans outside Walker Bros. store, Temple Row, 11th June 1957.

New Street, 1957.

Summer Lane, 1957.

Warwickshire's Eric Hollies, considered by many to be the finest spin bowler of his era, leaves the field for the last time in a championship match, County Ground, Edgbaston, 27th August 1957.

Alum Rock Road, 1957.

Coventry Road, Small Heath, August 1957. Note the man on the right, dressed in the height of fashion!

TODAY'S TV AND RADIO PROGRAMMES

HOME—330m., 93.5 Mc/s VHF

6.25 Market Report. 6.30 News Summary. 6.33 Bright and Early. 6.55 Weather. News. 7.10 Programme Parade. 7.15 Morning Music. 7.50 Lift up your Hearts. 7.55 Weather. News. 8.10 Programme Parade. 8.15 Weekend Shopping.

8.20 Morning Music (continued). 9.00 News. 9.10 Otters and Others. 9.25 Brahms. 10.00 "The Embarrass-

Skiffle Club—Light, 10 a.m.

ment of my Uncle Hamish." 10.15 Service. 10.30 News Summary. Music While You Work. 11.00 Time on my Hands. 11.30 News Summary, Music from the Ballet.

12.00 The Lou Preager Orchestra. 12.15 "The Archers." 12.55

Weather, News. 1.10 The Saturday Show. 2.00 Golf The Ryder Cup. 2.05 Desert Island Discs. 2.35 "L'Ami Fritz"—play.

3.05 "Maiden Steaks" —play. 3.35 B.B.C. Scottish Orchestra. 4.55 Golf. 5.00 Children's Hour. 5.55 Weather, News. 6.15 Town and Country. 6.45 Those were the Days. 7.30 In Town Tonight. 8.00 Variety Playhouse.

9.00 News. 9.15 Viscount Hailsham. 9.30 "French without Tears"—play. 11.00 News Summary, Weather. 11.08 Before the Ending of the Day.

BBC TV

11.00 The Ryder Cup—Golf. 1.15 The Ryder Cup: Motor Cycle Racing: Motor Racing at Oulton Park. 4.45 Children. 5.45 Today's Sport. 6.00 News Headlines and Weather. 6.05 Six-Five Special. 7.00 News Summary. 7.05 "Wells Fargo." 7.30 Dixon of Dock Green. 8.00 Variety Cocktail. 9.00 What's My Line? 9.35 The Phil Silvers Show. 10.00 Sports Special. 10.30 News. 10.45 Fougasse. 11.00 Weather; Viscount Hailsham (Sound Only).

LONDON I T V

2.00 Afternoon Out. 4.55 Brave Eagle. 5.25 Saturday Showcase. 5.40 Sports Results. News. 6.00 Abbott and Costello Show. 6.30 Charlie Chan. 7.00 Wyatt Earp. 7.30 O.S.S. 8.00 64,000 Question. 8.30 Saturday Spectacular. 9.30 Five Names for Johnny. 10.00 News. 10.05 The Private Life of Henry VIII. 12.00 Epilogue.

LIGHT—1,500m., 247m., 89.1 Mc/s VHF

7.00 Morning Music. 7.30 and 8.30 News Summary. 9.00 Children's Favourites. 9.30 News Summary. 9.55 Five to Ten. 10.00 Saturday Skiffle Club. 10.30 News Summary, Music While You Work. 11.00 Time on my Hands. 11.30 News Summary, Music from the Ballet.

12.00 The Lou Preager Orchestra. 12.30 News Summary, Transatlantic Song Book. 12.45 Sports Parade. 1.10 The Saturday Show. 2.00 The Novelairs. 2.10 Motor Cycling International Gold Cup Meeting. 2.25 The Novelairs (continued).

MIDLAND I T V

2.00 Afternoon Out. 4.30 Robin Hood. 5.00 Let's Go Shopping. 5.20 Cliffhanger. 5.38 Rugby League Results. 5.40 Sports Results, News. 6.00 Martin Kane—Private Investigator. 6.30 I Love Lucy. 7.00 Hour of Mystery. 8.00 64,000 Question. 9.00 Round the Rings—Wrestling. 9.30 Five Names for Johnny. 10.00 News. 10.05 You'll Never Get Rich. 12.00 Epilogue.

2.45 Motor Racing International Gold Cup Meeting. 3.00 Watch Your Step. 3.15 Bandstand. 3.45 Motor Racing.

3.50 Association Football. 4.45 Motor Racing. 5.00 Sports Report. 6.00 Guitar Club. 6.30 Just Jazz—records. 7.00 Radio Newsreel. 7.24 Association Football. 7.30 News Summary, Airs from the Alps.

8.00 Melody on the Line. 8.30 News Summary. 8.45 Film-Shows for Desert-Dwellers. 9.00 Saturday Popular Concert. 10.00 Carnival of Venice 1957. 10.30 News. 10.40 Richard Attenborough — records. 11.15 Take Your Partners. 11.30 News Summary. 11.55 Late News.

THIRD—464m., 194m., 91.3 Mc/s VHF

8.00 Orchestral Concert. 8.50 To Everything a Season—talk. 9.10 Orchestral Concert. (Part 2). 9.50 "Once More unto the Breach . . ."—talk. 10.15 Paisiello. 10.40 "Ideal."

NETWORK THREE —464m., 194m., 91.3 Mc/s VHF

6.30 The World of Books. 7.00 Record Review.

MIDLAND—276m.

1.10 B.B.C. Midland Light Orchestra. 6.15 News. 6.20 Sport in the Midlands.

WEST—285m., 206m.

8.20 Record requests. 1.10 News, Sporting Preview. 1.25 The Farmer. 1.50 Jazz Brief. 6.15 Sports Results. 6.27 Sport in the West. 6.50 Sports Results. 6.55 "At the Luscombes."

WELSH—341m.

4.25 "O Law I Law" 5—serial play. 6.15 Sports Medley. 6.50 News from Wales. 7.30 Teulu'r Mans: Welsh serial.

LUXEMBOURG—208m.

7.00 Saturday's Rejamboree. 10.00 208 Dancing Club. 10.30 Remembering Glenn Miller. 11.00 Bringing Christ to the Nations. 11.30 Record Round-Up.

A F N—547m.

7.00 Music in the Air. 8.30 Saturday Night Country Style. 8.55 Johnny Lee Wills. 9.00 Basin Street Jazz. 9.25 It's New. 9.30 Rock 'n' Roll Dance Party. 10.00 Music Views from Hollywood. 10.35 Dance Date. 11.00 Sports Night Cap. 11.05 America's Popular Music. 12.05 Late Request Show.

DISC of the DAY

MOOD MUSIC: Record shops are swamped these days with exotic LP titles of the "Music for Tired Lovers"—"Music For a Lost Weekend" genre. (The latest in America is "Music To Get You Into The Mood For Listening To Mood Music.") Some of them have been of indifferent quality, but three new ones are just the thing for that relaxed feeling: "Kenton With Voices" (Capitol 12in. LP) is a subtle blending by Stan Kenton's orchestra, a female voice and a male quartet; "A Fellow Needs A Girl" (Capitol 12in. LP) presents the imaginative piano playing of Joe Bushkin with a lush background; "Did Someone Say A Party?" (Brunswick 12in. LP) features Artie Shaw's clarinet playing.

You can ALL enter

The Birmingham Mail
HOME-MAKERS' COMPETITIONS

- OVER £300
- IN PRIZES
- NO ENTRY FEE
- 49 CLASSES
- SECTIONS FOR
- EVERYBODY
- CALL OR POST
- COUPON NOW

NOW IS THE TIME to register YOUR entry in these competitions. ENTRY FORMS MUST BE IN BY SEPTEMBER 18th, BUT EXHIBITS ARE NOT REQUIRED UNTIL SEPTEMBER 25th.

Prize-winning and selected exhibits will be shown at

The Birmingham Mail
MIDLANDS
IDEAL HOME EXHIBITION
Oct. 2nd — Oct. 26th

HOME-MAKERS' COMPETITIONS "The Birmingham Mail" 38, New St., B'ham, 2. Please send schedule and Free Entry Form to—

Name ....

Address ....

A SATELLITE is today circling the earth at a height of 560 miles. It is the first earth satellite ever launched. And it is Russia's.

It was launched yesterday, according to an announcement by Tass, the Soviet News Agency.

Mary Street/George Street, Balsall Heath, 18th November 1957.

Court Oak Road, Quinton, December 1957.

Balsall Heath Road/Longmore Street, Balsall Heath, December 1957.

The President of the Birmingham branch of the Inner Wheel,
Mrs. J.G. Skinner (second right), proudly displays some of the toys
collected for hospitals, 10th December 1957.

Christmas Party, BSA, Sparkbrook, c 1957.

Tyburn Road, Erdington, 1958.

The work goes on, modernising the buildings opposite the Odeon, New Street, 27th January 1958.

The Blues' Gil Merrick (sixth from left) presents George Peace and the White Hart Darts' Team with a cup, Aston Road, 1958.

As the poster says, Birmingham's own Anne Heywood is welcomed back at New Street Station, 6th February 1958.

Lower Priory, 26th February 1958.

Black Lane/Oxhill Road, Handsworth, 1958.

Eversley Road/Green Lane, Small Heath, 10th March 1958.

Warwick Road, Acocks Green, 17th March 1958.

Pershore Road, Stirchley, 11th April 1958.

Moseley Road, Moseley, April 1958.

Northfield Road, Harborne, April 1958.

Fazeley Street with Andover Street, right of centre, 1958.

The Albion cinema, Holyhead Road, Handsworth, 23rd June 1958.

Albion to play Villa at cricket

THE annual cricket match between Aston Villa and West Bromwich Albion will be played next Wednesday at Portland Road, Edgbaston (3.0). This will be the seventh occasion the match has been played, each side having been successful three times.

Aston Villa won the last game with a score of 154 for nine wickets against the Albion's 141 for eight wickets.

It is usual that each team bats for two hours or a complete innings, and the winners are the side scoring the most runs irrespective of the wickets lost.

There is not likely to be much change in the composition of the sides from last season.

It is hoped that Derek Kevan. and Derek Hogg, the new arrival from Leicester City, will be playing.

Ethel Street, 1958.

James Collins (Birmingham) Ltd. (brass founders) rear of Leamington Road, Erdington, 10th July 1958.

Worcester Street, looking up to New Street, 1958.

Martineau Street/Union Passage, 1958.

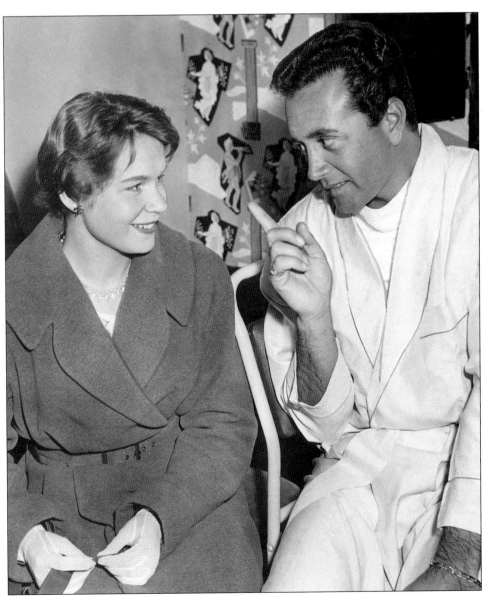

American recording star, Vic Damone, meets Nancy Cook from Moseley,
Hippodrome, 22nd July 1958.

Phil Silvers, as Sgt. Ernie Bilko, with men of his platoon in "The Phil Silvers Show", BBC TV, 25th August 1958. The show is just as popular today and re-runs are constantly shown all over the world.

Tommy Steele, appearing at the Town Hall, 30th September 1958.

Birmingham bandleader, Sonny Rose (left) meets American bandleader, Duke Ellington, 23rd October 1958.

Hawthorn Road/Kingstanding Road, 1958.

Singer, David Hughes, meets some of his old colleagues from Lawley Street Station. Hippodrome,
4th November 1958.

Angelina Street/Stanhope Street, Highgate, New Year's Day, 1959.

Weaman Street, 1959.

Worcester Street, with the back of the Market Hall on the right, 1959.

Conybere Street/Upper Highgate Street, January 1959.

Dennis Lotis and Christine Yates, starring in "Puss in Boots" at the Alexandra Theatre, 8th January 1959.

Moor Street, 1st April 1959.

Steelhouse Lane/Bull Street, 2nd April 1959.

Temple Row, with the site for the new Rackhams on the extreme right and Lewis's ahead, 1st June 1959.

Andover Street, 1st June 1959.

Washwood Heath Road, Ward End, 1959.

93

Summer Festival, St Oswald's Church, Dora Road,
Small Heath, c 1959.

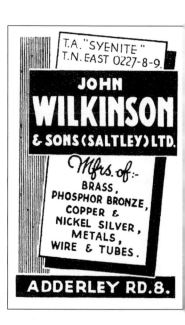

Suffolk Street, with Paradise Street at the top, 9th June 1959.

Lee Longlands (house furnishers), Broad Street, 24th June 1959.

Newhall Street, 26th June 1959.

Monument Road, Ladywood, 13th August 1959.

Monument Road/Wood Street, Ladywood, 1959.

Velvet-voiced American singer, Billy Eckstine, topping the bill at the Hippodrome, week commencing 24th August 1959.

Firemen tackle a blaze at the premises of W. Ogle and Co. Ltd., Gothic Arcade (off Snow Hill), 16th September 1959.

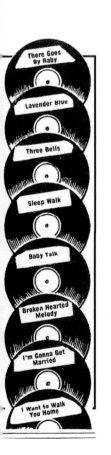

Bordesley Green/Bangor Road, 8th October 1959.

The Lord Mayor, Ald. J.H. Lewis, unveils the United Nation's Flag,
Council House, 24th October 1959.

Coventry Road, at the point where it runs into Cattell Road, Bordesley Green, 27th November 1959. The famous horse
trough was sited on the corner opposite.

Coventry Road, with Warwell Lane on the left, South Yardley, 3rd December 1959.

Horse Fair/Holloway Road, December 1959.

Back Cover: Great Western Arcade, 5th October 1954.

ACKNOWLEDGEMENTS

(for providing photographs, for encouragement and numerous other favours)

Keith Ackrill; Norman Bailey; The Birmingham City Council Dept. of Planning and Architecture; The Birmingham Post and Mail Ltd.; Alan Brewin; Carole Burton; Dave Carpenter; Jim Cross; Philip Haycock; Doug Hobson; Dave, Thelma and Tom Jones; Joyce Lockwood; Dennis Moore; Cliff Newman; George Peace; Anne Randle; Margaret Ryder; Bill Samuels; Keith Shakespeare; Ray Smedley; Rodney Smith; Hazel Steele; Ian Turner; Joan Wanty; Mavis and Jim Webber; Rosemary Wilkes; Keith Williams; Ken Windsor; Malcolm Wood.

Please forgive any possible omissions. Every effort has been made to include all organisations and individuals involved in the book.

The Green, from the tower of Kings Norton Church, 15th May 1957.